I Lost Everything

A Faith Filled Guide on How to Bounce Back from Divorce, Foreclosure and Repossession

Stephanie L King

I Lost Everything
Copyright © 2014 by Stephanie L King

ISBN (978-0-9905569-0-9)

Dedication

This book is dedicated to my husband, Tony and our three girls, Tatiyana, Gabrielle and Jasmine.

To my husband, I appreciate the Godly man and leader that you are. It is because of your dedication to the vision God gave you that we are where we are today. My life didn't really begin until I laid everything aside and joined you as your helpmate. I am forever grateful for your encouragement, love and support through sharing our testimony in this book.

To my girls, I know it has been a rough ride. I've asked you to hang on so many times while we moved from state to state, city to city and house to house. Following God is not always easy nor do we get to choose where we end up, but it is worth it! I am grateful to have had such incredible, sweet and loving children to share in this journey. I pray that one day as you grow older and read this book, that the words God speaks through me will encourage you in your walk with him!

Table of Contents

Preface

God spoke this book into existence. He wanted me to use my life as a testimony to his goodness. I can't take credit for anything but being obedient to his call. God gave me the story, experiences, wisdom and insight to put on paper. He told me to share my story and here I am. I give him alone all the glory for every word in every page of this book. I'm just the vessel but the truth is, these are his words.

I'm grateful for all the many people who poked and prodded me to get this book done because they saw a gift in me that I didn't recognize. I pray something that God speaks through me sticks to your soul and inspires you to bounce back!

"And everyone who has given up houses or brothers or sisters or father or mother or children or property, for my sake, will receive a hundred times as much in return and will inherit eternal life (Matthew 19:29)."

Introduction

Here you are, in the middle of losing something you think you can't live without. But, I'm here to tell you that you can. In fact, my life proves that life will go on after divorce, foreclosure and repossession. I would say that it gets better. But, you have a choice to make, do you sit there in self-pity or do you stand up boldly in the valley and proclaim the goodness of the God you serve. I chose God and he has given me a better life than I ever lost, a life of abundance, purpose and destiny! The same God I serve loves you too and wants to do the same for you. Are you ready to bounce back?

1

God Has a Purpose

When you find yourself in the midst of losing something significant to you, whether it is your marriage, house, car, or all of your personal belongings, it's hard to believe that God has a purpose. There is something in us that cannot comprehend that there is any good in our suffering. But, there is. The perfectly orchestrated events that you are facing are meant to propel you into a life you have never known before! This life, if you chose today to bounce back, will provide you with blessings and a purpose far greater than you can imagine. I've been where you are at the crossroads between depression and destiny. I chose destiny and am now living a life I could have never dreamed of. Will you join me? Hang on and know that your loss is just the beginning of your life in Christ. There is a purpose for your pain!

Appreciate Life

When you lose everything you once thought was important, there comes a time when you're forced to look around and learn to appreciate the life you have left. Loss is all too familiar to many of us. I know you may have just bought that car but it's gone. You thought you would raise your children in that house, but now someone else will. You just knew you and your spouse would grow old together, but instead they will grow old with another. Your mother left that jewelry to you when she died but now you're selling it just to feed your family. The stories, while slightly different, all bond us by one common thread and that is that we have all, in one way or another, placed too much value on something that can never fulfill the deepest desires of our hearts. When all of these "things," are gone, you have to start taking inventory of what you have left. If you're still waking up each morning and God has given you a chance to make your mark on this world another day then you have something to appreciate, your life.

The one thing that loss forced me to do is take inventory of what I had left. When I ended up on the low end of life where everything is gone and the days are a struggle to survive, I started to realize that I was in good company. There were more people there with me that was much worse off than I was.

At one point, my family ended up having to rely on state medical benefits. I can remember walking into one of the only doctor's offices that would take our insurance and the office was filled with people who were poor. But, even worse, a lot of them were really sick. I'm talking sick with cancer, walking with canes and children who had mouths full of rotted teeth. Suddenly, my "poor", pitiful self started to thank God that I wasn't in their shoes. I still had my health, my children had cavity free mouths and none of us were wondering if we would live or die tomorrow from cancer.

What about you? You lost your home, but do your children still have somewhere to sleep at night? They came to pick up your car, but do you still have money for food? Your husband walked out on you, but do you still have your health? Take inventory of what you have left and be thankful. The bible tells us to, "Give thanks in all circumstances..."(1 Thessalonian's 5:18). Praise God for what you have left, not only because that is his will for your life but also because when you really stop to think, it could be worse.

Your life on this earth is so short and uncertain that you don't have time to stay in this place of self-pity over what you've lost. Do you understand how incredibly blessed you are to have made it this long? Think back to when you were a child and you looked at the adults as "old." It didn't seem so long ago did it? Now you have arrived at what you once perceived as being "old" and just like a vapor you'll be gone too.

You have to appreciate every single day that you have life. God was gracious enough to let you wake up again this morning while thousands weren't so lucky. The longer you keep looking back over your shoulder at what's gone, the less time you have to appreciate the beauty of the moment you still have left. Don't "die" at this place. Live, even in the "ditches" of life!

Learn to Trust God

Once you lose something that you once believed was secure, it will make you question what really *is* secure in your life. Will your job keep you employed until you retire? Are you for certain that you will always be able to pay your mortgage or car payments? Are you absolutely sure that your spouse will never walk out on you? The answer to every one of these questions are no. There are so many variables that could change your life in a split second. But, what is secure and always will be is God. Sometimes, he allows us to lose what we perceive as everything in order to see that in reality *he* is everything.

Let's be honest with each other, we got so busy with our marriages and material possessions and acquiring those things that God just kind of fell to second place, right? I know you didn't place him there on purpose and sadly, if you were like me, you may have not even realized that you were doing it. But, God knew it. He watched as you placed your spouse, car, house, and "things" at the forefront of your mind and heart. God had to allow something drastic to happen in your life so that there was no question who should be first. He wanted you to stop looking around and start looking up.

The bible says in John 10:10 that, "The thief comes to steal, kill and destroy; I have come that they may have life and have it to the full." Nothing happens to us that God is not aware of. He allowed your loss so that you would take the things you valued the most off the throne and put him back on it. The only way you would be able to have the life he intended for you is by getting you to devalue those things and see that having life to the fullest would come through him. God is life. Nothing in this world can give you the life that he can through Jesus. He knew it but you didn't until he got your full attention.

Now that God has your full attention and you've realized that he is more important than what you lost, he needs you to learn how to have faith in him. Recall the story of Jesus in the boat (Mark 4:35). While the storm raged on, the disciples were afraid and Jesus was asleep. The disciples woke him and said, "Teacher, don't you care if we drown (Mark 4:38)?" Immediately, Jesus calmed the storm and asked the disciples if they really had faith. If they did, they would not have been so afraid.

I'll have to be honest, when I lost everything, I had many moments where I was just like the disciples asking God if he cared if I "drowned," in my struggles. It took many nights of crying myself to sleep, on my knees, praying to God for me to finally hear what he was trying to say to me. See, God wanted me to look beyond my boat that was raging against the storms of life and see what he sees. He does care. But, instead of being terrified of my storm, God wanted me to keep my eyes fixed on how powerful he is.

Once your eyes are fixed back on God instead of the storms you're battling, this is when he can really start to remind you of all of the times before when he has kept you. When you look at the bible, there are many amazing stories of how God delivered his people from harm over and over. God delivered Noah from the massive floods that destroyed all humankind on the earth. He saved

Moses from being killed as an infant by the Egyptians. What about David? God gave him favor over his battle with Goliath as well as all of Israel's enemies. God delivered his people from slavery and bondage in Egypt. Most importantly, he redeemed Jesus by raising him from the dead when he was crucified on the cross. But, none of these stories come without loss, struggle, trials and tribulations. You can't expect that your story will be an exception while you remain in this world.

Look back over your life. Think about all of the times God has delivered you. His track record is impeccable. While I was in my darkest hour, God started to remind me of all the many victories he had given me up until this point. There was the time he didn't let me die from a ruptured ectopic pregnancy or have cancer when the test results came back. Then there were all of those days growing up when I always had a place to sleep and food on the table.

What about you? I know there are also many times where circumstances could have been different had God not stepped in and delivered you. Take a moment to reflect on those things. Praise God right where you are. But, most importantly, remind yourself that if he delivered you then, he will deliver you now. Stop trying to solve everything on your own. Trust God to solve it, and have unmovable, unshakeable, faith while the storms are raging against your boat.

As you reflect on the situations that God has given you the victory over in the past, he will begin to show up in your present. Over and over during my loss, there were situations that God allowed me to be in that seemed impossible to get out of. But, I learned that we serve a God of possible.

When you are truly in the will of our Heavenly Father, you have to rest and give him the responsibility for your life. God says, "Come to me, you who are weary and burdened, and I will give you rest (Matthew 11:28). What he is really saying is lay your burdens on him, survive by his grace alone and that is where you will learn to live freely. Are you truly laying your situation in God's hands or are you still trying to solve it, waking up worried and laying down at night with a heavy heart? I urge you to trust God. Lay your burdens down and ask for his grace and strength to carry you through.

Overcoming Greed

God does not want us to live in greed. The book of Luke chapter 12 says:

"Then he said to them, "Watch out! Be on your guard against all kinds of greed; life does not consist of an abundance of possessions.

"And he told them this parable: "The ground of a certain rich man yielded an abundant harvest. He thought to himself, "What shall I do? I have no place to store my crops.'

"Then he said, "This is what I'll do. I will tear down my barns and build bigger ones, and there I will store my surplus grain. And I'll say to myself, "You have plenty of grain laid up for many years. Take life easy; eat, drink and be merry."

But God said to him, "You fool! This very night your life will be demanded from you. Then who will get what you have prepared for yourself?'

"This is how it will be with whoever stores up things for themselves but is not rich with God (Luke 12:15-21)."

Before I lost everything I owned, I would not have considered myself a greedy person. I always helped people around me when I felt they needed it. I would give my daughters clothes to other mothers who may have not been as fortunate as myself. At Christmas, I bought great gifts for others and I shared with friends when I had the opportunity at work.

If you had asked me, my name and the word "greed" would never have been in the same sentence together. But, according to Merriam-Webster dictionary, greed is defined as, "A selfish desire for more of something than is needed." To elaborate, greed is desiring more than what is needed, not to fulfill Gods purpose, but to fulfill your own. Based on that definition, I was, in fact, greedy. My entire focus was my family and myself. What was your focus before your loss? Did your marriage or money build the Kingdom or just *your* household?

My sole purpose in life before my loss was to get, get, get. I wanted to get the next promotion to get more money to get a bigger house and get a better car. My entire life consisted of getting more. The bible talks about the greedy in Isaiah 56:11 by saying, "They are dogs with mighty appetites; they never have enough. They are shepherds who lack understanding; they all turn to their own way, they seek their own gain (NIV)." Of course, this sounds a little harsh, but can you relate? I can certainly look back and see how it applies to me.

It takes a long look back at your life and a lot of self-realization to say you're a greedy person. No one wants to be labeled as greedy. But when you have an obsession with accumulating degrees, titles and things, like I did, more than you have an obsession with Jesus, you are, in fact, greedy. God loves you far too much to let you stay this way. He knows that, sometimes, the only way he can get you to look to him is to allow you to lose everything around you that is distracting.

What I realized is that I was obsessed with accumulating material goods and then I would give God the credit for them as an after thought. But, he didn't want just "credit" for giving me my own selfish desires. God wanted me. More than that, he wanted to use me to fulfill his purpose in the Kingdom. I can assure you that God needs you, too. He needs your time, attention, and worship.

When you're focused more on your marriage, house, cars and "things," than you are God, you can't develop the personal relationship with him that you need in order to carry out the calling he has on you life. God has to get your eyes and ears focused first on him so that he can change your heart to be open to helping build the Kingdom. In order to do this, you need to be focused on reaching others through unselfishly giving of your time, money, testimonies and talents. You can't do this if all of your time is devoted to gaining for the benefit of yourself and your family. Greedy people only go after what they want with no concern for anyone else. By overcoming greed, you can start to let go of your desires and instead take hold of the desires that God has for you.

Be Like Jesus

God wants you to be like Jesus. Did you know that? In fact, before he even formed you in the womb, he already knew that he was making you in the image of his son. I love how The Message version of the bible translates Romans 8:29:

"God knew what he was doing from the very beginning. He decided from the outset to shape the lives of those who love him along the same lines as the life of his Son. The Son stands first in the line of humanity he restored. We see the original and intended shape of our lives there in him. After God made that decision of what his children should be like, he followed it up by calling people by name. After he called them by name, he set them on a solid basis with himself. And then, after getting them established, he stayed with them to the end, gloriously completing what he had begun."

Wow. When you think about it, what an honor it is to be formed in the image of Jesus. He was sinless, patient, humble, giving and grateful just to name a few. But, even more than that, his number one purpose on this earth was to restore our relationship with God by being a sacrifice for our sins.

Your loss is part of God shaping you in the image of Christ. As painful as this sounds, it's not entirely about you. Sure, God wants you to have the best of life while you are living on this earth. But, more than that, he not only wants you to make it to heaven, he also desires that no one else should perish. He needs you to help Him do that and the best way to get you there is shaping you think like our Savior. "Since Jesus went through everything you are going through and more, learn to think like him. Think of your sufferings as a weaning from that old sinful habit of always expecting to get your own way. Then you'll be able to live out your days free to pursue what God wants instead of being tyrannized by what you want (1 Peter 4:2 MSG)."

If you look closely enough at the life of Jesus, you will realize that he traveled with little to nothing. Do I believe that God wants us to travel the world by foot with not a single possession to our name? No. But, I do believe as we look at the life of Jesus while on earth, we can draw an accurate conclusion that his life was in no means about materialism. God does not want our lives to be consumed with "things" either.

Jesus says to his disciples, "Sell your possessions and give to charity; make yourselves purses which do not wear out, an unfailing treasure in Heaven, where no thief comes near, nor moth destroys. For where your treasure is, your heart will be also (Luke 12:33)." I don't believe God is saying here that he wants us to live in poverty. If we did, how could we help build the Kingdom? It takes material resources to do that. We need money to feed the homeless, help care for the orphans and the many other assignments God has for us. But, what I do believe is that God is looking for radical people who cling to him and nothing here on earth, just like Jesus did; people that will follow him at any cost. People who are so detached from their "things" that if God said to give it ALL away, they would do it without a second thought. Are you that kind of person? If not, know that God is using this season of loss in your life to make you that way.

The entire reason that God sent his son to earth was to restore his relationship with humanity. Jesus was not on this earth to gain for himself. He was here to give himself for our heavenly Fathers purposes. Everywhere his feet traveled, Jesus set out to proclaim the goodness of God and build his kingdom.

As early as 12 years old, Jesus knew he was here to fulfill Gods purpose. In Luke chapter 2, the bible records a time when Joseph and Mary (Jesus earthly parents) had taken Jesus to Jerusalem for the Feast of Passover. After spending several days in Jerusalem, Joseph and Mary left to return home and did not realize Jesus had been left behind in Jerusalem.

"When they did not find him, they went back to Jerusalem to look for him. After three days, they found him in the temple courts, sitting among the teachers, listening to them and asking them questions. Everyone who heard him was amazed at his understanding and his answers. When his parents saw him, they were astonished. His mother said to him, "Son, why have you treated us like this? Your father and I have been anxiously searching for you."

"Why were you searching for me?" he asked. "Didn't you know I had to be in my Father's house (Luke 2:45-49)?"

From the age of only 12, Jesus knew his number one purpose was to be about his Father's "business". I can't even remember what I was doing at the age of 12 but I can pretty much guarantee it didn't have anything to do with proclaiming the goodness of God nor being remotely interested in anything he had to say. But, as we transition from childhood to adulthood, God wants the same for all of us, and that is for us to be on this earth and make him the priority.

We should be telling all we meet about our Father, all he has done for us, and the spectacular life he has waiting in Heaven for those who believe in him. But, when your focus is more on what you have accumulated in this life than what you have to gain in the next one, you have become more about your *own* business than our heavenly Fathers. When you look around and have nothing, that's when you recognize that your Fathers business is the only one that will never fail.

Jesus had a spirit of endurance. He had to learn to endure so that he would be able to with stand the storms that would rage against him. If he had not endured through the setbacks that faced him through his walk on this earth, he may not have fulfilled the plan God had for all of humanity through him. Where would we be without Jesus? His endurance saved our lives and your endurance is what will get you to the finish line of your own race.

In Matthew chapter 26:39, Jesus goes to Gethsemane with his disciples to pray. He was weary and found himself in a moment of weakness thinking about the crucifixion he was about to face. Jesus said to them, "My soul is deeply grieved, to the point of death; remain here and keep watch with me." And He went a little beyond them and fell on his face in the sand and prayed, saying, "My Father, if it is possible, let this cup pass from Me; yet not as I will but as You will."

My soul is deeply grieved, to the point of death? Wow, those are some very powerful words from the son of the living God! I felt his pain just reading them. You and I have lost some things and I can tell you my heart was grieved and my soul weary. But, being deeply grieved to the point of death, I cannot imagine.

Even after Jesus was so deeply grieved at the thought of his impeding death, he went back a second time and prayed, "My Father, if it is not possible for this cup to be taken away unless I drink it, your will be done. (Matthew 26:42)."

In this scripture, we see Jesus at one of his weakest moments; the moment where the burden of his life has weighed his soul down to the point of wanting to die instead of walking through the fire. We can all relate to some extent. In fact, you may be at this very moment in your life right now. But, what God wants you to see from the life of Jesus is that although his flesh was weak, his spirit endured.

During this time in your life, there are many things that you will just have to stand and endure. Often, when you begin down the path of loss, it starts as a raindrop and then turns into a violent tornado that destroys everything you once knew. There were days that I cried so much that I could barely see through the swelling and film of tears in my eyes. I had moments where I begged God to let me go "back" to where I had come from where my bills were paid, I still had my job, and a beautiful house to come home to. But, God wrapped His arms around me and gently reminded me that, "...in due time, we shall reap a blessing if we do not give up (Galatians 6:9)."

You too will reap your blessing if you endure this season. Lift your head from the loss, raise your arms toward Heaven, and receive the strength God is waiting to give you. Endure the times where everything you can think of is going wrong. Endure the days where you just don't feel like waking up and facing your life. Endure the moments where you are so weary that you can barely look your children in the eye without falling on your knees in utter despair.

Friend, God is refining your inward strength to with stand the stress to accomplish his best for your life. You have no choice right now but to just endure the tornado around you. The doors behind you will not open back up and the ones in front of you won't stay open forever. So, whatever you do, don't stand still. If you have to, you cry, crawl and claw your way to the finish line. But, whatever you do, don't dare give in!

Patience was and still is one of my hardest character flaws to master. I know God knew this when he allowed this period of loss in my life. I am a type A personality and if you know anything about us type A's, it's that we have to get things done now, now, now! But, Jesus was patient. This served him well because he waited 30 years before he even began his ministry. Even knowing his calling, he had to be patient and wait for Gods perfect timing to unfold.

Patience is accepting a difficult situation from God without giving him a deadline to remove it. Think about that for a minute. How many times do we pray, say we have "faith" that God will deliver us from a bad situation or give us guidance but then start getting frustrated when nothing happens in what we deem as a "reasonable" time? I can tell you that I am still struggling with this. Oddly enough, the only thing that has helped me to become more patient is to be in more situations where God tests my willingness to wait on him.

Hebrews 6:12 says, "We do not want you to become lazy, but to imitate those who through faith and patience inherit what has been promised." One would assume that based on this verse, you don't inherit the promises God gave you unless through patience. Jesus knew this and God wants you to develop patience while you face this trial.

I remember when we were down to absolutely nothing. I mean nothing. My husband and I, both type A personalities, former military and "go-getters," were literally sitting around watching entire seasons of TV shows day in and day out. We were waiting on my husbands military disability claim to go through. Minutes felt like hours, hours felt like days, and days felt like years. Oh, just thinking about that time makes me cringe. We were waiting on the Lord to come through in our favor on this disability case for over a year! My husband couldn't work because of his disability, I couldn't work because I was pregnant and it aggravated my back and we tied all of our cash up in an investment property that wasn't selling.

When I look back on that period in my life, I can see clearly that God was developing my patience. He allowed me to be in a place where I had no choice but to wait on him. There was absolutely nothing I could do to fix the situation, make it go faster, or rush his timing. I just had to wait.

I know it's difficult to sit there watching everything crash around you with God whispering in your ear, "Just be patient." But, what I can tell you is that these times of forced patience will become some of the most important times on your walk with the God. He will speak to you, teach you and prove to you that he can be trusted. These are the days you will draw upon when you find yourself in troubling waters again. It will happen. This won't be the last of your struggle. The difference is, the patience you are developing now will allow you to have an unsurpassing peace during your storms later.

Be grateful. I know you may not want to hear that but it's a hard lesson God is trying to teach you in order for your heart to become more like Jesus.

You can say you are grateful. But, the test of finding out if you are really grateful is when all your "stuff" is gone. The hardest thing to do is be in the midst of loosing everything and still praise God for what you have left. When you really think about it, your "nothing" is "everything" to someone else. What they are praying for, you still have.

Five loaves of bread and two fish; that's all Jesus had to feed five thousand men, women and children. Can you imagine being in the situation where you had to feed all of those people with that small amount of food? I know you can imagine it because there are some of you that are looking your children in the face right now and you barely have enough to feed them.

Jesus could have complained. He could have just said it wouldn't work. He could have been angry with God for putting him in what seemed like an "impossible" situation. But, instead, he told the people to sit down, then he looked toward Heaven with the little amount of food he had in his hand and gave thanks. He gave thanks. That's it. Jesus was grateful for the little he had and trusted that God would provide the rest.

Until you can look towards Heaven and give thanks for *your* "five loaves and two fish," God will not open the doors for more. Your gratefulness will unlock more blessings for you than anything you could work for and provide on your own. He can do more with your "nothing" in an instant than you could do in a lifetime. All it takes is one God moment to completely change your life!

God has something better in store for you. But, the biggest blessings are not for the faint at heart. Perseverance helps overcome the greatest difficulties. The only way you can learn to persevere is by being put in situations that test your ability to achieve success despite delay and difficulty.

Job was a man of perseverance. He lost his ten children; livestock and servants all in one day, but still worshipped the Lord (Job 1:13-19). Then when he was struck with sores all over his body, his wife encouraged him to curse God, but even then, he refused. God saw that Job persevered through his darkest hour and yet was still faithful. Because of this, Job was given double for his trouble.

I remember when we were in our darkest hour. Everything was gone, twice in a one-year period and I was pregnant with my third girl. My husband woke me up at 2AM one morning when the last car to our name was being repossessed. I was so weary from the weight of everything else on our lives that I couldn't even process what had just happened. All I could do was cry myself to sleep, again.

When I woke up that next morning, I refused to feel defeated. I knew that if I had given up in our darkest hour that I may never recover from that moment. See, God had already given me the vision of the promised land. But, I knew I would never make it there if I didn't continue on despite the difficulty. My perseverance gave me the fuel I needed to push through to the promises of God.

If you can just persevere through your pain and the weight of the process, God will see to it that your faithfulness was worth it. You have to believe that he has something better on the other side of this valley. But, if you stop half way during your climb up the mountain, you will never manifest the double reward God has waiting for you!

Loosing a marriage, all of my money and every material possession I owned was the best thing that ever happened to me. I really mean that. Before the loss, I was a wandering Christian blinded by the greed of myself. Now, I am closer to God than I have ever been. I have a compassionate heart. Most importantly, I have purpose.

You have to see the greater good in all of this. Although you can't "see" two feet in front of you right now, this is the time where you put your hand gently into the hand of God and let him guide your every step. Fight to overcome the greed you didn't realize you had. Grow closer to God by learning to trust Him in your darkest hour. Let God shape your heart and mind to resemble the heart and mind of Jesus. I promise, once you rest in the process, God will do all the work while you do all the waiting. he will show you that there is a purpose for all of this pain!

2

I've Been There

I've been there; right where you are, divorced, broke, and weary wondering where God was. I wanted to know why he let me work so many years against all odds to build this incredible life only to watch me lose everything? He was the one who told me to walk away from all that I knew for the "promised land." I was obedient. I followed with a faithful heart. I was excited. Why would he forsake me? No matter how you made it to this point, we have something in common; I've been there. I lost everything. But, I'm also where you are headed, in a land where blessings overtake me and purpose pursues me.

Let me start by saying that I in no way was raised with a silver spoon in my mouth. I grew up in a home where my parents were divorced and we lived with my grandparents. The house we stayed in was around 1,000 sqft and on any given day, I shared a bedroom with my mother and brother while other family members were scattered amongst living room couches and the floor. Don't get me wrong, I appreciate that I even had a place to live. But, I grew up wanting more. I always felt a fire inside of me to break through the chains of poverty.

In addition to the crowded living conditions I endured, there were also many days of violence and instability in our house. On a regular basis, my uncles would come in drunk or high and be ready to argue with whomever was willing that day. As a young child, it was always so frightening for me to see the pure anger that poured out of the hearts of my family. I recall many times hiding in my bedroom closet, in tears, fearing that someone may end up physically getting hurt. The police were regulars at our house and so was the devil. It was the only explanation I had for the hate that seemed to always surround us. While children my age were eating Sunday dinner with their families, surrounded by love and peace, my life was a living nightmare.

There was one day that I can remember where my mother wanted to go out for the evening with her friends. For whatever reason, my grandmother didn't want her to go. As she walked out the door, I stood there and watched my grandmother drag my mother to the ground and punch her over and over. All I could do was stand there and feel sorry for my mother in fear that if I ran to her defense, I may also feel the wrath of my grandmother's anger. My soul was just empty and I longed for normal.

Poverty, violence and instability weren't the only childhood troubles I fought to overcome. Have you ever watched someone take his or her last breath from cancer? I have. As a child, it isn't something you should see. But, I did. My uncle was healthy one minute and just months later; he was lying in our back bedroom turning yellow and dying from colon cancer. I watched a healthy young man, full of life and dreams deteriorate to a lifeless body that had no choice but to accept his fate. The day he died, I sat on the floor with my grandmother. As he took his last breath, she held his hand crying while my mind just went blank. I believe at that point, I had just become numb to everything bad. It was the only coping mechanism I had. If I let myself feel the real pain of my life, I might have never recovered. Although I know God was with me, I didn't "know" him yet.

The most difficult thing I can remember ever having to overcome was the suicide of my favorite uncle. Out of everyone around me, I saw myself in him and I believe he saw a piece of himself in me too. My uncle was a smart guy who had left our small town for bigger and better things. I remember him calling from time to time to check on my grades and how I was doing in school. He was the closest view I had of what making it "out" looked like.

All I remember was seeing everyone around me become hysterical in an instant. "They have the S.W.A.T team up there on Danny!" The chills from that moment still follow me to this day. My uncle's fiancé had left him and he attempted to commit suicide by taking a massive amount of pain pills. At some point, when the damage was done and he was hysterical, delirious and drugged from the medicine, my uncle took his fiancés father hostage, made his way to a hospital, (we believe to get help) and bit his ear off. He finally let the man go, ended up in the stair well negotiating with the S.W.A.T team but later died from an overdose.

I still remember that day vividly, the smell, my emotions and the emptiness in my soul. The day my uncle committed suicide, a piece of my hope died. I just couldn't understand how he could survive such hell growing up and then let life get the best of him. From that day forward, I knew I would have to fight to get out all by myself.

By the time I reached my junior year of high school, I couldn't take another minute of my life. I decided to graduate a year early and move on to the next chapter. So, I did. After surviving insurmountable odds growing up, I sat in the front row of high school graduation and walked the stage one year early as an honor graduate. Thank God for grace. That's all I can say for why I made it that far with a sound mind. Any expert will agree that my life was a statistic and excuse for why I should have been on drugs, pregnant or just lost. However, I proved them wrong.

After high school, I stayed around the area for a little while and tried college. But, at that point, God was calling me for more. Somehow, he orchestrated for me to bump into an Army recruiter while I was getting a flat tire changed. Amazing how God does that, huh? I was the farthest thing from Army material. In fact, I know many people, including my family, laughed at me and just knew I was going to fail. Talk about God using the most surprising of people for his toughest jobs. But, all he was looking for from me was a yes. So, two weeks after I met the recruiter, I was on my way to basic training and then to my permanent duty station in Hawaii. Looking back, I believe Hawaii was Gods way of rewarding me with a trip to paradise for all that I had endured as a child.

Hawaii was a blessing but it also proved to be another place of heartache when I met my first husband. Alone and empty, I met him at the young age of 21 when I had no idea what I needed in my life or what God wanted for me. I faced much more pain that I had to with him but I married him anyway in the hopes that he could fill a void that only God can.

After spending four years in the Army, I began yet another chapter of my life working in the Federal Government. It was during this period that God showed me tremendous favor as I worked my way up very quickly. After only 4 years, I had reached my mid twenties was married with one child, making six figures, owned a $300,000 home, great credit and I was a "top performer" expected to climb even higher. From the outside looking in, I had it all. Unfortunately the view from the outside did not reflect the hell which was going on inside.

Although I had spent years of my life overcoming odds that would knock the average person to their knees, I finally came face to face with a giant that I could not beat, my marriage. Having spent the first half of my life in a nightmare, I longed for the peace, stability and love that a mother-father home would provide for my daughter and me. Unfortunately, after fighting 7 long years to make it work, through infidelity and domestic violence, I gave in to the reality that my dream of that perfect home had just crumbled around me.

For the first time in my life, I felt defeated. What I thought was a reward from God to give me the peace I so longed for was just another "thing" in my bucket of broken dreams. But, I knew I had to keep moving. I felt that tug in my spirit that God had something big in store right around the corner.

After taking some time to heal from a broken marriage, I opened my heart to the possibility of love again. I'm so grateful I did because God blessed me with the man he had for me all along. When I met my current husband, I finally understood why I had to close the book on the chapter before. He was more than I could have imagined in a partner and came into my life with tenderness while showing me the love of Christ. What I didn't know is that God placed us together because he knew we would need each others strength for what was before us in the days ahead.

Meeting my second husband changed my life, literally. He walked into my world with a passion for God so large that it inspired me to be a better person. Suddenly, I left my days of "luke-warm" Christian behind and drew closer to the God that had kept me through hell all of those years. Up until this point, I knew God but not on the level he needed me to. As I began to draw closer to him, he drew closer to me. Many times over the previous ten years, God had asked me to do some pretty radical and risky things. However, this next one beat them all.

"Quit your job and support your new partner in his pursuit of the "promised land." Sounds just like something right out of the story of Abraham right? These were the words God whispered to me one night while I was watching a church program with my husband. My husband had been given a vision of creating wealth for Gods Kingdom through real estate. Now, as crazy as it sounds, when I look back on that moment, there was absolutely no question that I had to do it. I had no second thoughts, no nervousness and absolutely no doubt. Every other time in my life that God told me to do something daring, radical, and risky, I never hesitated. However, this time was different. This time, I walked so blindly into the unknown that even I look back and think about how crazy I must have looked to everyone around me. There was no plan, no job lined up and not a lot of security in the bank. All I had was knowledge of the vision God had given my husband and the word from the Lord to "go." So, blindly I went. But, not into the promised land as I so excitedly thought; God led us straight into the wilderness.

After receiving the word from God to walk away from my job, I put in a 30-day notice and began planning with my husband how we would tackle the challenge before us. Building a business is no easy task. But, we just knew that God told us to do this and he would help us through. However, we wanted to ensure we could make it without the steady income we both had walked away from. So, we moved into a small apartment and rented out the homes we both owned. Neither of us had enough equity to sell, so we figured this was the best option. We packed up all that we owned, downsized, stored what items we wanted to keep and sold or gave away the rest. Thinking we had it all figured out, we were ready to embark on our new journey!

Not long after we moved into our apartment, we came across a real estate deal. After carefully calculating the investment costs and profit we went for it. The numbers made sense and we just knew

God had led us to this. But, we ended up spending more to rehab the house than was budgeted for. We thought this would be a quick sale, quick profit, and quick return of the money we were living off of. But, it was far from that.

Our investment property sat on the market way longer than expected. This caused us to have to use our savings to live off of. However, because of the amount of money we had to put into the property to sell it, there wasn't much of our savings left. The only option we had was to start living off of our credit cards. Up until this point, our credit was still good as we were maintaining all of our bills on time. That soon changed. Our credit cards were maxed out quickly and we had to stop paying everything that was not necessary for us to live. In the blink of an eye, our credit went from perfect to poor and we were barely able to buy groceries.

Once we had depleted our savings, maxed out our credit cards and sold everything we had in storage, there was nothing left but what we had in our apartment. The only way we could make it was to use the rental income from the houses we had rented out. We were desperate. I knew that the family who was renting my home would soon be moving out, so instead of taking their rent and paying my mortgage payment, we used that money to live off of for the last three months of the lease.

This obviously started the foreclosure process on my home, as I was unable to catch up the payment. So, instead of letting the bank take what I had worked so hard for, I initiated a short sale. I wanted to at least keep some of the small amount of dignity I had left.

Soon after I lost my home, I had to also call the bank to pick up my car, as I could no longer afford the payment on it either. At this point, I had lost everything. Not too long after everything we owned was gone, our investment property finally sold. Although we didn't make nearly as much profit as expected due to holding costs and unforeseen expenses, we did have our original investment money back in the bank.

My husband had heard from God that we should move to the Dallas area. The real estate market there was much better than where we were investing in Toledo. So, off we went with our oldest daughter and brand new two-month-old baby again in pursuit of "The promise land."

Once arriving in Dallas, we felt that our troubles were over. Another word from God to leave everything behind and money in the bank, we just knew he had something great in store. What we didn't expect was to once again lose every penny we had. After moving costs, deposit on our new rental home and savings for living expenses, my husband had a plan to use the remaining amount to get our real estate business up and going. Long story short, that didn't go as well as expected and there we were again, barely able to pay the bills.

How in the world could God let this happen to us again? We said yes to everything he told us to do and believed without a doubt in our mind that he would provide for us. But, little did we know that right around the corner God was planning to give us back double what we had lost. I'm so grateful we didn't give up.

Shortly after, God started supernaturally opening up opportunities for our business. First, he opened up a job opportunity up for my husband. At that point, we were grateful to be doing anything that brought income in. We had to take a step back while God was moving things around for us to jump ten steps forward. It was amazing, one door after the other started opening up for us. After all of the devastation, it was incredible to see the supernatural blessings start to overtake us. There was absolutely no doubt in my mind that God had his hands in everything coming our way. Although the road to this point had not been easy, it was starting to be worth it!

Just three short years after losing everything, we are now living in a 5,000-sqft house with two new vehicles, two out of our three children in private school, money in the bank and our real estate business taking off like we can't believe. We're making double what we walked away from! There is no way that we can take credit for all that is happening in our lives. We would never have been able to accomplish where we are had it not been for the favor of God on our side and our faith in him. God has surely restored everything and more that we lost.

After fighting my way through a childhood filled with poverty, violence and instability, I had finally made it to what I deemed as "successful." But, what I learned was that when you are a child of God, his definition of success has a far greater meaning than your own. When God told me to walk away from everything I had worked so hard for, I thought that he would have something better "instantly" ready for me. But, as I so quickly found out, God's ways were not my own and I lost everything. However, after gently and lovingly guiding me through the wilderness, he restored more than I lost. But, the most important thing I gained was a passion, purpose and calling to serve the Lord through my pain.

3

Dealing with Embarrassment

To say that I was embarrassed to be divorced and completely broke is an understatement. But, what this process made me recognize is that I was not alone and there were things far more important than what other people thought of me. Now that you understand a little better why God may be allowing this to happen in your life, I'd like to give you some practical advice that I learned along my journey that will help you deal with the embarrassment you are likely facing.

First, let me put something into perspective for you. The only thing that matters in your life right now is that you are still blessed to be alive and on the road to your destiny. Personally, I recognized that I was healthy, my children were healthy, I still had access to food and water and a place to lay my head at night. You are in the United States of America where you can get help and any dream in your heart is within your reach. You may not be where you used to be, with whom you used to be with, but you are on the road to where God has called you to be. You shouldn't be embarrassed, you should be proud to be chosen.

When I was pregnant with my second daughter, my husband and I had moved into a 936-sqft apartment. This was when we thought we were being smart by downsizing to reduce our monthly bills. We knew building a business would be hard and we needed to keep as much money as possible. Coming from a 2400-sqft house that I owned by myself, this was no place I wanted to invite my family to.

I remember planning to bring my daughter home to that apartment and realizing that I didn't even have a nursery to bring her home to. I was so embarrassed of the circumstances that I did all I could to ensure none of my family drove in from out of state to witness the birth of my daughter. The day I had my baby, I'll be honest, I had a low moment wishing I had my family there to share in that joyous occasion.

What I realize now is that the people who matter, the ones who love you with or without a husband, job, big house or money, won't care what you don't have anymore. Figure out who those people are and let them in on what you're going through. The rest of the people are just bystanders in your journey and won't help you one bit on the road to your destiny. Who cares what they think? You don't owe them an explanation, answer, or an open window into your life. Keep your eyes on God.

Instead of even being remotely concerned about caring what other people will think or say about you, focus on what's going on inside your household. Chances are, if you have children, they know more than you think they do. If you have a spouse, he or she is likely more stressed out than you know. You are not in this alone. This is the time when you need to show your children that in spite of losing material things or another parent in the house, that they are still loved and safe.

I remember the day my ex-husband and I told my then 4 year old little girl that daddy would be moving out of the house. Just talking about it brings me right back to the moment where I fought to hold back the tears trying to be strong for my daughter. I'll never forget the look on her face when she started crying and said, "But Daddy, who will watch cartoons with me?" Heart breaking is an understatement.

In that very moment, nothing or no one else mattered. Embarrassment was the furthest thing from my mind. All I saw was an innocent child who just had her entire world flipped upside down in the matter of a minute. The last thing I cared about was what people at work would say, who in my family would have something to say or what some unknown person down the road would say about a "divorced" single mother. All that mattered was helping my baby through one of the hardest moments in her young life.

Chances are, if you haven't already told your children what's going on, you will soon have to tell them something. Stay focused, as you will need every ounce of strength and attention to get them through this. If you don't have children but you have a spouse, you're both going to need to come together during this time as a team and lean on The Lord. If you have neither, then recognize that you are not in this alone. The bible says, "Blessed are those who mourn for they shall be comforted (Matthew 5:4)." God is standing right there beside you and will not leave nor forsake you.

Embarrassment is a very public emotion that makes you feel exposed and regretful for the circumstances you're going through. You tell yourself that in relation to society (people such as the next door neighbor or your co-worker) that you have failed to maintain the level at which you "should" be operating on. In order to be embarrassed, you would have to compare yourself against a "status." But, let me tell you a secret, the "status" that God has for you is far greater than the one you are comparing yourself to right now.

At one point, I was embarrassed that I no longer had my big house, my six figure "important" job, great credit, on and on. But, looking back, I shouldn't have spent a single minute thinking about any of that. See, God was trying to get me on his level, the one where there were not only material and financial blessings like I had never known before but also purpose and destiny.

You can only be embarrassed if you keep comparing yourself to others. Look at it this way, you might have thought you "made" it living in that neighborhood or snatching that husband that all the ladies seemed to have wanted. But, God knew you weren't even scratching the surface to where he has planned for you. This time right now is only a setback for your setup. Where you're going is far greater than where you thought you made it. But, sometimes you just have to take two steps back to make a giant leap forward.

Embarrassment is an emotion from the enemy. See, he wants to keep you held down by this unnecessary feeling so that all you focus on is what you lost instead of what God has for you to gain. He wants you to compare yourself to what your friends, family and neighbors still have so that he can make you feel like God has abandoned you or that you are a failure. Learn to recognize this trick from the enemy and actively tell yourself that this little bump in the road is not embarrassing, it's just a necessary part of the road to your destiny!

If I went out on a limb, I would guess that at least 99% of people worldwide have or will be embarrassed at some point in their lives. Recognize that everyone holds some level of embarrassment over something they wished hadn't happened. It could be as "small" as tripping at high school graduation or as large as having the neighbors watch the repo man come drag your car out of the driveway. Maybe you were at the country club or in your social group bragging about how great your marriage was and now you are divorced.

Whatever your embarrassing moment is, don't let your perception that you are the only one keep you from holding your head high. Chances are, those people you think are laughing or talking about you are very well going through something in their home that they are hiding behind closed doors. If they aren't now, at some point they likely will be. Everyone, and I mean everyone, will face some type of unexpected hardship in this lifetime.

One thing that truly helped me get over being embarrassed is looking past my emotions and taking inventory of the situation. Yes, I was divorced. But, I wouldn't be a "divorced" mother forever. This was just a required step to move on from the man I chose for myself and open the door to the man God intended for me. Yes, I lost my house. But, I knew I could rent for a little while until things stabilized again, be a better steward of my finances and purchase another home in a few years. Yes, my credit went from perfect to poor but credit could be rebuilt as soon as that situation was under control. Focus on the possibilities of where you can go from here. You can't be embarrassed unless you dwell on where you are at this tiny moment in your life.

Find something to laugh about. I know you might be rolling your eyes at me right now. But, I promise, the more you laugh, the less likely you are to dwell on what you've lost nor have time to be embarrassed over it. Turn on a comedy show on TV, go spend some time with that funny friend you have, or spend time with your kids tickling them and letting their laughter make you smile. If you don't want to do any of that, then go straight to a mirror and make the most ridiculous faces at yourself. If that doesn't get you laughing, I don't know what will!

Here is probably the most important piece of advice I can give you when it comes to being embarrassed, go visit the homeless. When we moved to Texas God placed it in my heart to help the less fortunate. We were just getting back on our feet but would still take the time to go down and give them sleeping bags or a home cooked meal. You want to talk about being embarrassed. Talk to someone who is digging through trash to find his or her next meal. There was one lady who would not receive what I was trying to give her nor would she even look me in the eye. I didn't take offense to it; I just assumed she was ashamed and embarrassed to be that situation.

See, what you perceive as embarrassing would actually make someone else proud. How? While you see it disgraceful to lose your home and have to downsize and rent, someone homeless would be proud to have any place at all to call their own. Even if you are going through a divorce you can see the brighter side. Some woman out there is getting severely abused by her husband and doesn't have the courage to walk away for fear that he will kill her. She would be proud to be able to move on with her life and children as a strong woman all on her own.

Your life is what you perceive it to be. Don't always look around at the people in your circle. Sometimes, look back at people who would give anything to be you, who are trying their best to get to where you are, even in these horrible circumstances. That alone should encourage you that you are blessed and should be proud to hold your head high in spite of losing it all! Today is the day you forever erase embarrassment out of your mind, heart and vocabulary. In the life of a child of God, we don't waste time dwelling over what we've lost, we "...press on to reach the end of the race and receive the heavenly prize for which God, through Christ Jesus, is calling us (Philippians 3:14)." Right? So, press on!

4

Let Go

So, here you are, at the point of no return. This is the moment where you deal with what is and look forward to what will be. But, in order to do that, you'll need to let go of what was. In this chapter, I'll walk you through the stages of grief and loss and share with you how you can move on. Remember, you can't look forward and backward at the same time. You can choose to stand there looking over your shoulder at what's gone or you can look straight ahead to what is coming.

First, don't deny reality. By that I mean wake up (in the nicest way). If your husband has left you for another woman, has already moved in her house, is out partying with the old high school friends every night and doesn't answer your calls or text messages, its over. Really, it is. And why in the world you would want to sit around hoping things will get 'better,' with someone who has moved on with their life, I don't know.

I remember when my ex husband and I were nearing the end of our marriage. I had found out at work that he was cheating on me (again). When I met him at home that evening, of course I was devastated, crying my eyes out. But, did he care? Absolutely not. His mind, head and heart were with another woman. Here I was bawling my eyes out about how hurt I was and all he could say was, "Are you done? I don't want to talk about this ever again after midnight?"

Are you kidding me? That was the only thing that kept running through my mind when he said that. There was no further emotion left for me, or any amount of respect. I knew it was over.

Although it took me another few weeks to gain enough courage to ask for a divorce, in that moment, I accepted that the marriage was over. Thank God I did because what good would it have done me to hang on to someone who left me a long time ago?

The same thing goes for your job, house, car or other material possessions. If you have done all you can to save that house, by that I mean tried to get a second job, worked with the bank to renegotiate your payments or tried to borrow the money and it still just isn't working out, then get out of there or initiate a short sale. It will be easier on you and your family if you walk away voluntarily instead of being forced out by the sheriff.

You cannot truly move forward with your life until you accept that what was, no longer is. Can you think of any time in the past that you have ever held on to something longer than you should have? Now, can you think of any benefit at all you got out of it besides to not do it again? This time is absolutely no different. Take a moment to accept what was lost. If you have to, write it down on a sheet of paper, look at it, read it out loud, cry over it (quickly), then rip that paper up and throw it away! You know it's over, gone and there is no going back. Time to make it official!

Next, what you need to be very careful of is that you don't let what you lost make you angry. This is another trick from the enemy that will keep you trapped in a never-ending roller coaster of emotions. The bible cautions us many times against anger because God knew there is no good that can come from it.

Proverbs 37:8-9 says, "Refrain from anger and turn from wrath; do not fret--it leads only to evil. For evil men will be cut off, but those who hope in the LORD will inherit the land."

Notice it said, "…it leads only to evil." How many of you have heard of stories on the news of exes killing their former significant others and then turning the gun on themselves? Then we learn that they had two young children in the home while it happened? What a preventable tragedy. I can almost guarantee that anger was at the root.

See, the moment you choose to hold on to anger against another person is the day you let the enemy claim territory in your heart. You can't let love in because it can't reside with anger. Let me say that again, love cannot reside with anger. When you hold on to anger for losing a person or losing a thing, you cannot show love in the manner that God intended you to, whether it's towards him or another human being.

There are so many times I have had to catch myself from being angry at my ex husband for his disregard to our marriage vows, angry that he wasn't concerned about me or the effect his actions would have on our child and angry that he never said sorry. To be honest, I still struggle with this today. The only thing that keeps me from letting that anger creep back into my spirit is by conscious prayer every time I have to deal with him.

Once you recognize that you are holding anger against anyone, for anything, open your mouth and say this, "I refuse to let anger reside in my heart. I am a child of God and will walk in love as he commands. I know the enemy will try to block my future blessings by making me walk in anger, but I refuse to give in to the tricks of the enemy!" Sometimes, it takes actively recognizing your anger and actively fighting it to let it go.

Listen, sitting around depressed over what's gone won't help you and it certainly won't move you one step closer to your destiny. Do you realize that every moment you waste another day lying in the bed, locked in the house that the world around you is still moving (without you)? You aren't promised the next minute, so don't waste the one you do have sitting in a negative emotion. Someone in the grave would love to trade places with you. So, why would God give *you* another day when you're sitting around depressed and not grateful to be alive? What are you doing for *him* today?

There were quite a few days where I started to throw myself a pity party. It's easy to do when all you do is focus on the negative. But, I learned pretty quickly that I had control over my mind and emotions. The minute I recognized that negative emotions were starting to take root in my mind, I turned my favorite gospel station on Pandora radio and just started praising God.

See, when you focus your mind on praising God for all of the good he has done in your life, there is no room for depression to take root. It never failed, every time I turned on my praise and worship music, I always felt better. I was able to take on whatever came my way that day because my mind was focused forward on the possibilities of life. If you aren't into music, then pray & praise God, and do it over and over until you feel better.

Depression is a feeling of sadness and hopelessness. But, you are a child of God with so much in store for your life. There is no reason to be sad for what you lost because what's ahead is so much greater. When you have the God of the entire Universe directing your path, there is absolutely no reason to feel hopeless.

"The righteous cry out, and the Lord hears them; He delivers them from all their troubles. The Lord is close to the brokenhearted and saves those who are crushed in spirit.

The righteous person may have many troubles, but the Lord delivers him from them all; He protects all his bones, not one of them will be broken (Psalm 34:17-20)."

Put your faith and hope in God, not your things and other people. When you truly rest in faith, your emotions won't be so tied to "things" but in Gods ability to do what is best for your life. Depression can be a devastating emotion if you don't get it under control quickly. Don't throw your hands up and rest in such a permanent emotion during a temporary situation. Yes, this is temporary. In the grand scheme of your life, this is just one tiny moment that is a necessary detour on the road to your destiny!

Now that you've let go of what you lost, lets take inventory of what you have left. I know you may say nothing, but that's not really the truth. Only those who are in the grave have "nothing" left and even then, they have gained eternal life. So, you can find something right now to be grateful for.

Grab a piece of paper and write down every single thing you are thankful for. Take inventory of what you have left whether it is material, relationships, health or anything else you can think of. If you can't think of anything, let me remind you. You are still alive, you have the intellectual ability to read this book and you may be sitting in a home and not on a park bench.

What about your job do you still have that? Do you still have your children with you in spite of your divorce? If not, I can assure you that you are in a country where there is a justice system, which will grant you rights to continue to see them. Do you still have access to clean water and food? If you say you have absolutely nothing left, my response is that you still have Jesus. That alone is enough. That alone has secured your relationship with our Father and given you access to eternal life. Now, whether or not you choose to be grateful for that is up to you, but you always, always, always have something to be grateful for.

Here I was, sitting in a small apartment, and just had my second daughter. We sold everything we possibly could get money for out of our apartment and storage. There was nothing in the bank. We paid only the necessities at that point and barely had enough to get groceries. I remember we were on our way to Thanksgiving dinner and our gas hand was almost on empty. So, my husband and I started scraping together pennies we had in our car to get gas.

I was so grateful to have had those pennies left. I'm so serious. In that moment, we may not have had much else but at least we had pennies left to get us enough gas to get to where we were going. I just praised God the entire time. And guess what, once we got to Thanksgiving dinner, our Aunt Ann gave us a $100 check! She had no idea what we were going through or the fact we had just scraped up pennies to make it there. It was just another example of how our praise & gratefulness for what we had left unlocked more of the blessings God had for us.

Once you have truly let go of what you lost and taken inventory of what you have left, you can now look forward to what you have to gain. The bible says in Isaiah 61:7, "Instead of shame, you will receive a double portion, and instead of disgrace you will rejoice in your inheritance. And so you will inherit a double portion in your land, and ever lasting joy will be yours."

Do you believe that? I do because I am living it. I don't wish for a single thing back that I lost because the husband I gained is so much more incredible, the cars I gained are so much better, the lifestyle I have now is one of freedom and the home I gained is honestly double in size from the one I lost. But, most importantly, I gained a compassionate, grateful, giving heart and now I serve the Lord so much more fervently than I did before.

If God has restored my life so much greater than what I lost, he can do the same for you. I am not famous, I didn't come from a rich family and believe me, no one I know has "connections" with anyone important. My only true source is God and I give him all the glory for what he has done through me. Peter said it perfectly in Acts 10:34 when he said, "I now realize how true it is that God does not show favoritism."

Let it go, take inventory of what you have left and look forward to what is ahead. It sounds easy but it will take active work on your part to stay aware of your emotions and actively fight anything negative that tries to take root in your heart. Most of all remain grateful for what you have left. When you've truly stopped trying to pry back open the door to what is gone, you will be more aware to the doors God is swinging wide open on your behalf, the ones that will propel you into your destiny!

5

Bounce Back from Divorce

In the society we live in, divorce has become such a common word. But, to those who live through a divorce, the experience feels anything but common. If you let it, divorce can spiral your entire life out of control. Having been where you are, I can assure you there is a brighter day and a new spouse waiting for you that will make you grateful for this time in your life. Before you get there, though, there is a little work to do. In this chapter we'll talk about how to not only survive the dreaded divorce but also how to regain control of your life and look forward to a brighter day.

Here is some news in case you didn't know; the divorce rate in America alone is roughly 50%. According to USATODAY, 2.189 million people are expected to get married in 2014. That means approximately 1.09 million of those people will end up divorced at some time in their lives. That's just for one single year. Now, do you feel alone? You shouldn't.

First, pause for a moment and accept that your ex-spouse was not the person God intended for you. I can tell you for sure that the spouse God intended for you won't walk away, they will love, honor, cherish and fight for you. They can't leave you for someone else because the other part of their soul is with you. They will know you're the person God placed in their life and although they'll make mistakes, there will be no doubt that there is no one on this earth, besides you, that they are destined to be with. The feeling will be mutual. You can't divorce your soul mate. So, lets accept that this person was not that.

I met my ex husband when I was 20 years old. Well, I should say 20 years young. At 20 I didn't have a clue who I was, where I was going or what I wanted for my life. More importantly, I didn't know what God wanted *for* me nor did I even consult him through prayer to ask. I was just a wandering young girl in search of someone to make me feel loved and secure.

The first thing I recognize and accept when I look back on the mishap of my first marriage is that I did not consult with God on when and who he wanted me to marry. I tried to fit with someone who wasn't supposed to fit with me. My ex-husband wasn't a believer at that time and I was. The bible says, "Do not be bound together with unbelievers; for what partnership have a righteousness and lawlessness, or what fellowship has light with darkness (Corinthians 6:14)?"

I do remember when I was discussing marriage with my ex-husband hearing this bible verse as a "whisper" in my spirit. But, I chose to ignore it. I thought I could change him into a bible loving, devoted, Christian man. It was not to say I was any better than him but God knew the path I was on was one of righteousness and being paired with an unbeliever that wasn't quite there yet would do me no good.

When I met my ex-husband, I was a young soldier in the Army and all alone in Hawaii, with no family or friends. I think more than anything, I was just lonely. I met him, fell head over heels in love (or so I thought it was love), and was soon faced with one of the most devastating times in my life.

About 6 months after we met, I was pregnant and afraid. It just so happens, right before I told my ex husband, I had also just found out that he was cheating on me. This would be the first of many times. Although, I think the first time is always the most devastating. Don't you agree? You put so much hope and faith in this person to love and cherish you only to find out that all they are is a flawed human being, just like you. It's almost as if you make them "God," hoping they will love you perfectly and unconditionally for the rest of your life. The older I get, the more I realize that only God himself can provide that kind of perfect love.

About 5 weeks in to my pregnancy, I started having unusual bleeding. So, my ex and I went to the doctor to find out what was going out. It turns out that they could not locate the baby in my uterus. At that point they suspected an ectopic pregnancy but couldn't be for sure and sent me home to be monitored (by my ex). An ectopic pregnancy could kill me if it ruptured my fallopian tube and I bled internally without quick medical intervention.

As I lay in the back bedroom afraid of the unknown, devastated at the thought of the loss of a child, I sat there lonelier than I have ever been. See, in one of the scariest and devastating moments in my life, my ex husband sat in the living room of that apartment giggling and joking on the phone with his new girlfriend (the one he cheated on me with).

I can remember the tears rolling down my face as I prayed and asked God for forgiveness. I knew in my heart I shouldn't have ever been sitting there. Had I listened to that whisper in my spirit, I wouldn't be facing such a devastating moment.

Can anyone relate? I'm sure every one of you reading this can relate in some form to that same feeling of despair.

The next day, as I started having terrible cramps, my ex husband rushed me to the emergency room. Turns out I did have an ectopic pregnancy which had ruptured my fallopian tube. The doctors had to do emergency surgery as I bled internally near death. I'm so grateful for the angels surrounding me that day. I came out of the surgery with one less fallopian tube, no baby, but alive to face another day.

When I woke from surgery, I was grateful that my ex was at least there. I figured bad company was better than no company. To his credit, he did stick around to make sure I was ok. I'm glad he did as I don't think I was strong enough at that point to get through it alone.

After my ex broke up with that new girlfriend and realized the great woman he had in me, he came back on bended knee, and of course I let him back in. Sounds just about as quick and easy as it was in real life. Lord, what was I thinking. Now, I *know* I am not alone on making crazy decisions right?

My ex-husband and I were married six months after we met and ended up spending seven long years together. Those were seven of the most difficult years of my life. Time after time, I stayed with him through the cheating, lying and roaming the streets. I even stayed after he got drunk one night and punched me in my face over and over while I was 11 weeks pregnant with our daughter (yes, you heard me right). What's even worse is that *I* apologized to *him* the next morning for getting him angry enough to hit me. Oh how painful it is to look back at that woman who didn't love herself enough to walk away.

Up until the day I asked my ex-husband for a divorce, I didn't even consider it. I was a fighter. I was an overcomer. I refused to give up. All I wanted was a stable and loving home for our daughter. I thought if I fought hard enough that he would come around. But, he never did and to be honest, the marriage was so far damaged that I don't believe I could have ever trusted him again no matter how hard he tried. It was just a matter of time before I let go of what never really was.

They say women fight for so long but once we get to the point where we are tired of fighting that there is no returning from that. For me, that was the truth. One day while I was at work, a few weeks after his last cheating episode, a sudden peace came over me. In my spirit, I knew it was time to close that chapter of my life. Looking back, I also know it was God whispering to me that he had something better up ahead. I didn't have any idea how things would turn out for my life and I didn't have a man waiting for me on the side. It was just God, my daughter and I. But, I had faith that everything would be ok.

I called my ex husband on the phone and told him we needed to talk once we got off work. When I met him at home that evening, and told him I wanted a divorce, as mean as this may sound, I felt an overwhelming peace and relief in my heart. As I sat there watching him cry, everything human in me wanted to say all of the mean things he said to me as he watched me cry all of those years. But, the Christian in me just felt sorry for him. I apologized because I knew I could no longer be the wife he needed (not sure that I ever was). I couldn't be that wife to him because God had created me to be the wife and helpmate only for the man he created for me. My ex husband was never that man.

Not everyone reading this will have the same peace that I had regarding your divorce. For some of you, the news of a divorce was so sudden and devastating that you still can't believe its happening. But it is. Your divorce is really happening and let me be the first to tell you that this may very well be one of the best things that will ever happen to you. It certainly was for me. It was a door closed so that I could move forward to the glorious door God had waiting for me with the most loving and amazing man on the face of this earth (well, at least I think so).

I want to help you get through this because I know how heartbroken you feel right now but I also know the good that can come of it. You can't see it but I'm on the other side of this valley excited for you to discover the real life God has waiting. Trust me, one day, you'll want to call your ex every day and just thank them for pushing you towards the partner God designed especially for you (I promise).

So, I suppose you might already know what I'm going to say next, although you may not want to hear it. You need to truly forgive your ex for everything you are holding on to that they have done wrong. I'm not saying that you will forget, nor am I saying that by forgiving you are condoning their behavior. What I'm saying is that in order for you to move on with your life and make space for the many blessings ahead, you have to clean out the garbage of unforgiveness in your heart.

Forgiveness is a choice you make in obedience to God. In Colossians 3:13, the bible says, "Bear with each other and forgive one another if any of you have grievance against someone. Forgive as the Lord forgave you." It won't be easy and I'm certainly not telling you that you have to run to your ex and let them know that you have forgiven them. Maybe one day you can do that. But, for today, make an obedient and conscious choice to forgive.

Take a moment to write down all of the "things" you believe your ex spouse did wrong to you. After you have written down your list, pray this prayer over it:

"Father, I come to you with a list full of hurt. But, I want to be obedient to you Lord so that my heart may become more like Jesus. I am actively choosing to forgive my ex of these offenses against me and I pray that they, too, will forgive me for any wrong that I may have done as well. Give me the strength to move on with my life and into the destiny and purpose which you have called me."

Once you have laid aside your unforgiveness, it's time to get to know you again. After you've given so much of yourself to a marriage, sometimes, there is a tendency to become someone you don't know. I always said that my ex brought out the worst in me. I really believe that is the true test as to whether or not you should be with someone.

So, who are you? Start by remembering that person you were before you met your ex spouse. That could have been many years ago for some of you or just last year for others. But, no matter how long ago it was, just think about some of the good things you liked to do alone or with a group of friends.

Two things that I always found myself doing alone, before I met my ex-husband, was working out and reading a good inspirational book. Somehow, when I got married, I got so wrapped up into the marriage, hurt, and betrayal that I forgot about me.

Remember you today. If you don't have anything you used to like to do, what would you like to do now? What makes you smile? Where does your mind take you in the middle of a daydream? If you can't think of anything, go to the park or the beach and just marvel in Gods beauty. It's ok; I know the thought of doing anything "alone" scares you. But, ask yourself, how many times have you already been alone, even with your husband or wife laying beside you or sitting next to you at the movies? Where they really with you in body, mind and soul?

While you're getting to know you again, stay connected to God. For some of you, that will mean getting in to a good divorce support group at church. For others, it may be best for you to read a few inspirational books alongside your bible or even take up journaling. Whatever helps you stay connected, do it, and do it consistently.

Right now, God has you exactly where he needs you. You are in a moment of your life where you have no earthly distraction of a partner. You can focus on the word of God, stay in prayer and listen to him for direction on the next phase of your life.

God really does love you and he wants to be your first husband. The bible says, "For your maker is your husband—the Lord Almighty is his name—the Holy One of Israel is your Redeemer; He is called the God of all Earth (Isaiah 54:5)." Spend time praying, worshipping and spilling your heart out to him. Take this time to fall in love with God again because he has, and will continue to Love you. Death will never separate you from the love of God.

Now that you no longer have a marriage to focus on, its time to make a list of personal goals. Maybe you still haven't finished that degree you always wanted or started that new hobby that interests you. Whatever it is that you need to get done, it's time to sit down and write out your list.

One thing that has always helped me in goal writing is the "SMART" method. Your goals should be Specific, Measureable, Achievable, Relevant and Time-based. Take a moment to further research this method on the Internet and then get started writing your list of goals. Even if you only have one right now, it gives you something to work towards and less time to dwell on your situation. Walk in faith towards it and let God do what you can't by yourself.

Whatever you do, if you have children, make sure you pay attention to them. Chances are, they are just as heart broken as you are but don't know what to do about it. Children need stability and love. When they perceive one of those things failing with the stability of a two-parent home, they will need you to reassure them of both. Many of you are already used to being a single parent even while married. But, I'm sure you can think of at least a few things your ex-spouse provided to your children that they will miss by no longer having them in your home.

Now, here is the best advice I can give you about getting into another relationship, do what your heart tells you to. Many people will tell you not to rush and many others will try to get you out to the club at the first chance possible. But, move on when you are truly ready.

If you aren't healed, placing God first in your life, and working on you, it's likely that you aren't ready. All you will do by moving on to someone else right now is bring a lot of baggage with you. More than that, you will always be looking to that next person to be your 'savior,' and fix parts of you that only you and God can do. When they can't do that, you'll be let down by love once again. That's not the kind of relationship God intends for you.

For me, it didn't take me a long time to open my heart again to receive new love into my life. I always say that I never was really married to my first husband to begin with. By that I mean, the marriage wasn't real and sincere. I had a bad boyfriend who I just so happen to put on paper was my husband. The bible says, "Husbands, love your wives, just as Christ loved the church and gave himself up for her (Ephesians 5:25)." I never received that type of love from my ex-husband. He wasn't capable of that with me because he wasn't meant for me.

I started to date again about 6 months after my ex-husband and I officially separated. This time I was different. This time, I knew exactly what I didn't want and more of what I needed. I was stronger, more connected to God. and more importantly, healed from all of the baggage of my first marriage.

I met my husband now and when I tell you God is faithful, please believe me. Where my ex treated me as an afterthought, I am now treated like a Queen. Because my husband is a man of God, he takes his role as the head of our household seriously. He consistently keeps our marriage at the forefront of his mind and heart while ensuring God remains at the head. He opens doors for me, holds and reassures me when I have a bad day, drops everything he is doing when I need him, and kisses me softly just for no reason at all but that he truly adores me.

Until I met my husband, I never knew what it meant to be loved like, "Christ loved the church." Now, I know it means to be loved without limits or stipulations. It means to be loved through faults, bad days, and disagreements. It means that his love for me comes before himself and that if he had to lay down his life for me that he would. It's the kind of love that inspires me to be better, do better, and serve others more. It's the love God designed especially just for me before he ever placed me in my mothers womb.

Listen, I know your heart has been broken. I understand your dreams have been crushed. I've felt the pain of divorce. I have cried the same tears and felt the same emptiness in the pit of my soul wondering how I will go on. But that wasn't the spouse God chose for you, it was the one you chose yourself. The spouse he has for you won't give up on your love. I can't promise that they won't hurt you; every human has the capability to do that. But they will stay in it and fight with you. They will love you through your imperfections and through the pain of your past. They will inspire you to be better, not bitter. You should feel the love of Christ when they love you. If you don't, turn and walk away this time around. Don't leave this decision to yourself again. Let God decide because your destiny depends on it! You don't have time to waste repeating the same mistake. The love of your life is counting on you to leave the next one to God!

6

Bounce Back from Foreclosure

I've heard many times that your home is where your heart is. But, I found that home is wherever you make it. It can be in the house you worked years to purchase or the apartment you rented for 6 short months. Having lost my house too, I learned how to make home wherever my family and myself ended up. It's not over for you. If you have a desire to own a home again, know that it can be done sooner than you think.

Before the market crash around 2008, the word "foreclosure" was such an ugly word. Today, it seems like you hear it every time you turn on the television or pick up a newspaper. According to Realty Trac, just between 2007 and 2011, there were roughly more than 4 million completed foreclosures and 8.2 million foreclosures that were just starting. You definitely aren't in this alone.

When my husband and I downsized to an apartment, we had no intentions of losing both of our homes and 4 rental properties. We did the right thing and had tenants occupying each place so that we didn't have the added expense of those payments. On the rental properties, we were even making a few extra hundred dollars per month, which helped. However, even the best intentions can end up in troubled water.

It seemed like one thing after the other started falling just like dominos. After our investment property sat on the market forever, we maxed out our credit cards and blew right through savings. At that point, we were desperate. We started using the rent payments we were given by our tenants to pay our own bills, buy groceries, and just try to make it.

We knew what we were doing was wrong. Not only were we in a bad situation, but we were putting other families in desperate situations as well. Sometimes, especially when you are trying to provide for your family, there is no easy right answer. There are mistakes and there are things you would take back if you could. All we could do at that point was pray that God deliver us financially as soon as possible so that we had a way out. We also prayed that he would bless us exponentially so that we could bless others.

Needless to say, we ended up losing one house and the rental properties to foreclosure. The other house I initiated a short sale on. I figured it would be better in the long run on my credit to have a short sale. It was also better for my mind because it was as if I voluntarily handed over something that had been such a source of pride for me. During this time of losing my house I really recognized how deep I had been attached to "things." It was almost as if I was so proud of my stuff that I forgot about God.

Having been where you are, let me tell you that the first thing to do is realize this situation is just a temporary setback. I promise you it is. A foreclosure or short sale does not damage your credit so bad that you can't recover. You will rebound if you do the best you can as quick as you can. For now, just focus on making it through each day.

So, you may be losing a 4,000-sqft home or a 1,400-sqft home. Whatever the size, you can recover later. For now, downsize as small as you can. Don't worry about the lifestyle you had or what people may say if you went from a mansion to an apartment. Your main focus should be to live within your means at this moment and rebuild to the means you left.

I lost a 2,400-sqft home during the summer of 2010 while living in a 936-sqft apartment. This year (2014), we just moved into a 5,000-sqft home that we are purchasing. I don't say any of that to brag but only to show you what's possible by being smart on what you do from here and having faith that God will restore more than what you lost.

Right now, don't focus on buying right away. Focus on being stable, rebuilding your credit, bank account, and most importantly, your relationship with God. "Seek the kingdom of God above all else, and live righteously, and He will give you everything you need (Matthew 6:33)."

Once the dust settled on losing all of our properties, my husband and I knew our credit was going to be horrible. We could have sat and cried over it but what good would it have done. Instead, we praised God for what was gone and praised him even more for what was up ahead for us. We knew we had to have faith but we also knew that we had to do our part as well.

The first and most important thing to do is try your hardest to be the best tenant you can be. It's likely for a while, at least a couple of years, you will be renting. Most landlords know that people who rent usually don't have the best of credit (which is why they're renting). But, they don't want to deal with a tenant who doesn't pay their rent on time. That's why it's so important that you only rent what you absolutely know you can afford right now. Also, most banks that loan after foreclosures and short sales want to see an on time payment history for two previous years of your rental period. Bottom line, pay on time (early if you can) and be the best tenant you can be.

I remember when we were moving to Dallas and I was so worried about putting in an application to rent a house. I'm serious, I worried and worried about what the landlord might say, what if they don't accept us, on and on. But, God whispered to me, "Keep me first and I will work on your behalf." And he did. Surprisingly, the real estate agent who ran our application approved it with no questions asked and just a normal deposit. I was stunned. But, knowing the God we serve, I shouldn't have been.

There were several other houses we rented after that, before we moved into this one. Each time, I would feel a little bit of worry creeping in. But, then I remembered what God did before and I knew if the house were meant for us, God would take care of it. He kept reminding me over and over that because we were placing him first in our lives that he would open doors and make a way where it looked like there was no way. He proved to me each time that he controls everything. We were never turned down for a house we wanted to rent, although our credit was horrible. About the worse that came of it was that on one place, the landlord wanted a deposit and the last months rent.

If you're paying your rent on time and taking care of the place you're in like it's your own, there should be no problem with getting a good referral from the landlord. To be honest, not every landlord we dealt with even called previous landlords to confirm anything. We provided them proof of on time payments with our application, maybe a quick explanation of why our credit was less than perfect, and that seemed to suffice for getting approved.

Once you're stable and paying your rent on time, start focusing on your credit. I can tell you from experience that the number one most important thing you need to make sure you are doing is making on time payments on any back taxes and student loans you have. Both of those can be set up on installments based on income. But, as soon as you possibly can, get those paid on time. Those will certainly be conditions the bank will put on your loan.

You should also pull your free credit report from annualcreditreport.com. What will hurt you the most after the taxes and student loans are the accounts that are currently being reported as open and delinquent. Sometimes, the creditors write off your bad debt and leave it alone, and sometimes they sell your account to a credit collection agency. First, make sure that if the credit collection agency is now reporting a delinquent balance on your credit that the original creditor is showing a balance of $0. Then, contact each of the collection agencies to find out what the settlement amount is on that account. If it is something you can save in a reasonable time, hang up the phone and start saving. Contact them again once you've saved the payoff balance. If you can't settle in a reasonable amount of time, then set up a payment plan as low as you can until you can save the money to settle. This will at least show the mortgage company that you are recovering financially and trying to be more responsible on your accounts.

Here is a word of "Christian" advice regarding the very nice people at the collection agencies (some of them really are); don't let the devil use them to get you angry. They are trained to be pushy and get as much money as they can for the company they work for. Not to mention, they work on commission and are struggling just like you are to provide for their families. They are not superior to you because they're calling you about collecting a past due debt. I've had some call me a "deadbeat," while literally cussing at me, and others have threatened that their company is going to seize everything I own by suing me in court (good luck with getting nothing from nothing right).

Each time I dealt with a collection agency, I would pray before I called. Yes, I'm serious. No matter how pushy, loud, or annoying they got, I stayed calm. All I wanted to know was what my options were. Then, I politely told them to have a great day and I would contact them to set up a payment once I was able to pay. Do not let them play on your emotions or push you into making a payment when you are not financially ready. Remember, right now, stability is the key.

Now, when I tell you this, I have to make sure you know that I am not a credit advisor, accountant or any other type of financial professional. I'm just passing on what I did and what worked for me. There are company's out there who make bad credit loans. Yes, you will pay way more in interest on what you purchase but they report on time payments to the credit bureaus, which you need. Personally, we used a company called Crest Financial to finance furniture for our house. We were ok with paying a high interest rate so that we could rebuild our credit. They didn't even perform a credit check. If you use this company, try to keep the account open and make on time payments for at least 6-9 months of the 12-month loan. After one was paid off, we even went on and opened a second one just to boost our score a little more. You can also try to open a secured credit card from just about any credit card company out there. This will also help boost your credit.

What helped me the most on my credit to be able to qualify for a home loan was to focus forward. By that, I mean, opening the accounts mentioned above and paying those on time. To be completely honest, I didn't even worry about going back and paying all of the old accounts I was delinquent on. Almost all of them were written off as bad debt and just remain as a "ding" on my credit that will eventually fall off.

What you want to make sure that you are doing is showing the bank that your negative credit history was just a short window of time in your life under abnormal circumstances. Show them that you can be trusted now. If your situation is more complex than mine, you may have to file for bankruptcy. That's ok too! I know of people right now who also purchased 2 years after a bankruptcy. It's not the end of the world and may very well be what you need to start fresh. Get with a good company that specializes in bankruptcy and credit to better understand your options.

There are a couple of more things the bank will look at heavily before they approve you for a home loan. First, make sure that you build a stable employment history. Try to stay at one job before you even begin to start looking for another one that pays higher. If you do happen to start looking, make sure that you're staying in the same line of work. Banks look negatively on unstable employment. If you're self-employed, most all banks will need to see a copy of the previous two years of your tax returns. Keep in mind, the more deductions you claim, the less income you will have to qualify with when it comes time to apply. Banks look at your income after deductions, not just the amount of gross money you have coming into your business. Also, there are many types of mortgages out there. Chances are if you have had a loan before, you will likely be purchasing using a conventional loan with around 5% cash required to put down. Save two times that amount and keep it in the bank consistently for at least six months prior to applying. This will show the bank that you have strong cash reserves and are a less risky borrower.

Like I stated earlier, all of our properties were gone to foreclosure or short sale by the fall of 2010. In 2013, we applied for a mortgage and qualified with a credit score of just 590 & 620 (with Carrington Mortgage). All they asked for was an explanation of all of the delinquent accounts on our credit. We also qualified with a rent to own program (Hyperion Homes) which allows you to pick out the home you want, they purchase it cash, let you rent for 1-3 years and then you have the option to purchase with a traditional mortgage. These are only two companies out there that work with damaged credit. Do your research and use whatever company works best for your family.

When I say that you won't be where you are forever, let my life be an example of what can be restored. I not only gained a better home than what I lost, but I grew in my relationship with God because it took lots of work and lots of faith to get here. But, if I can do it, so can you. The point is to not let where you are right now keep you from where God is trying to take you. You can rebound from a foreclosure. For right now, remind yourself that your home is where you and your family are, no matter where that may be. The Lord was with you in the place you lost, where you are now and he will be with you in the next one. Jesus said, "In my Fathers house, there are many mansions: if it were not so, I would have told you. I go to prepare a place for you (John 14:2)." If God has mansions waiting for us in Heaven, why would he not provide a home for us here? Walk towards it in faith, excitement and expectancy!

7

Bounce Back from Repossession

It's just a car. Really, it is. There are millions of people all over the world who will never see a car in their lifetime. However, whether you realize it or not, you still have an opportunity to rebound and even sooner than you may think.

Towards the end of 2010, I could no longer afford the payment on my vehicle. So, I called the bank and told them to come pick it up. Luckily, we were still blessed to have my husband's car. But, all that came of my voluntary repossession was that they sold my SUV at an auction and sent me a collection notice for the remaining $1600 that was still owed on the loan. I didn't have the money to pay that and we both knew it. After they continued to contact me for several months, the bank finally wrote that amount off as a loss. I've never heard from them again.

By the end of 2011, things got much worse. The last car we had to our name was repossessed at 2AM one morning while I lay in bed asleep with our baby and pregnant with another one. I'll have to say that not having a source of transportation was certainly shocking. I had not been without a vehicle since I was 15 years old and at this time I was 32.

There wasn't really much we could do after our last car was repossessed. We contacted some veteran's agencies that may be able to assist us in paying the balance we owed. But, for a while, we were just stuck, left to figure out how to survive without a car. So, let me say this to you, I completely understand how devastating it is to not have transportation to get you to the store, work, or your children to school.

I believe losing our car was the moment the enemy thought we would give up. It was for sure the lowest moment in our journey through the wilderness. How would we survive? What would we tell our children? How could we get groceries? We lived in Texas, which was thousands of miles from our friends and family on the east coast. So, we literally had no one to rely on but God and ourselves.

We did what any other person would do who never had a car; we walked and used public transportation. More than that, we praised God that we still had legs left to walk with! It wasn't easy walking my daughter a mile to school because the bus didn't have enough room for her, nor was it easy watching my husband walk to the grocery store and come back with busted veins in his arms from the weight of the groceries. But, we weren't laying in the bed paralyzed, or in a coma at the hospital down the street, or locked behind bars at the local prison. No, we were still blessed and free to walk the earth like thousands of people have, and still continue to do today. Not having a car is more of an American problem than it is a tragedy.

After several weeks of not having a car, walking, and using public transportation, we were finally able to pay the bank what we owed on the past due balance and pick our car up at the repossession lot. To say that we were grateful is an understatement.

At the beginning of 2013, just 1.5 years after the second repossession, we qualified for a loan to purchase another vehicle. Then, at the end of 2013, we were blessed to be able to purchase a second vehicle, which was a 2012 Mercedes Benz. As the car dealership delivered this car right to my front door, all I could do was praise the Lord and think about the moment when the repossession company came to take our car. God is just so good isn't he? To top it off, just last week (2014), we traded our van in (just a year later) for a new one! God will restore!

So, how did we do it? Well, I certainly believe the favor of God stayed with us as we exercised our faith, praised him in the lowest moments, and were grateful for what we had left. But, there are a few practical things you can do right now to do your part. Remember, faith without works is dead.

First, recognize, again, that this is just temporary. It may take some months or it may take a year but soon enough you can be driving a car again. If you let the enemy get in your mind at your lowest point, you can never focus on what you have to do in order to claw yourself out of this hole! But, while you are in this hole, praise God for what you *are* still able to do. We weren't able to call a family member for a ride, but, praise God, we were still able to walk. For that alone I am grateful! Find something to thank him for right now.

If you do have to walk, ride the bus or catch a ride with your friend or neighbor, than just do it. Again, it's only temporary and you may just lose a few pounds, make a new friend or be able to catch up with a family member who needs to hear from you. While you are doing any of the above, praise God the entire time. In fact, if you run into a stranger, share the love of God with them. Now *that* will make the devil mad! It's all in your perspective. You can either be angry in this moment and make yourself miserable or you can shine your light in all of those places you would never be right now if you had your own transportation. Maybe God has a purpose in this too, right? You never know whom you can encourage just by a kind word.

So, I'm sure you are wondering just how we qualified for a loan so quickly. Well, it's a simple as this (really). We applied for a loan with an online car loan company called Road Loans. They specialize in giving loans to people with damaged credit and repossessions. In fact, we secured a zero down payment loan, with horrible credit. Again, any "credit expert" or financial advisor probably wouldn't recommend these types of companies because you will end up paying more in the higher interest rate. But, I'm not a professional expert. What I am is a real person who went through real bad times, just like you, with real children and real places to go. So, I had to do what I had to do to survive. Sometimes the good advice isn't always what's practical for real life. Do your research, pray and figure out what's best for your family.

After you qualify for a new loan, only take on a payment you know for sure is in your budget right now. In fact, be frugal and get a car that is below your means. Make the payments on time each month and within 6 months to a year, you can shop around to refinance that loan to a lower monthly payment and less interest charges.

If you don't qualify for a loan yet, then you can just continue on with walking or public transportation until you do, or you can save to purchase the car cash. It may not be the best of cars but it will do until you can get back on your feet again. Just put back as much as you can afford from each paycheck and before you know it, you can go buy a used car.

We actually purchased a car with cash before we ended up getting a loan to buy new ones. At that point in time, we were grateful for that second car! It wasn't the prettiest, but we felt like we were riding around in luxury! Compared to walking, it was heaven sent! When it came time to buy another car that was more reliable, we were able to sell our car online and get most of our cash back out of it. It was another great reminder in working hard and being grateful for what we had.

I know losing your only source of transportation can be devastating. But, it's really not that bad and it's really not your only source of transportation. Realize that this moment in your life is only temporary and the faith you place in God along with your praise and works can get you back behind your own wheel in no time! For this moment, let Jesus take the wheel and trust that he has better in store!

8

Destiny Awaits

Your destiny awaits. But, it won't wait long. The doors behind you are closed, what you've lost is gone, and the doors in front of you won't stay open forever. God has better in store for you. Do you see it or are you so attached to what was that you are blinded from seeing what he wants to give you? You've made it this far.

You've taken all of the heartache, disappointment, and stress for this long. Can you really afford to give up now or will you keep marching on towards the prize as a good soldier in God's mighty Army? Whatever you chose today, know that there is destiny and purpose on the other side of your loss. I made it and so can you!

You will always have trouble while you're in this world. If it isn't the loss of a job, marriage, house or car it will be the death of a loved one, illness of a friend or just the day to day pressures of living life. It almost seems as if when you start moving towards God, all hell breaks loose!

When I tell you that everything that could go wrong in the past several years, did, that is nothing but an understatement. I've just briefly given you a glimpse into what I faced financially. But, what I didn't mention is the fact that I was trying to raise three children on top of that who literally didn't sleep well for 3 solid years and stayed sick most of the time, or the addiction I was responsible for helping other family members overcome, or that while I was pregnant with my third daughter that my grandparents both died within six months of each other and I couldn't afford to get to their funerals.

See, the enemy knew I was walking towards my destiny. He saw what was on the other side of this mountain and figured if he threw everything at me at once that I might throw in the towel and give up. He wanted me to be discouraged and believe that God had abandoned me and that I should return to that lifestyle of mediocrity. But, the bible says that, "In this world you will have trouble. But take heart! I have overcome the world (John 16:33)."

Knowing that Jesus came to this world and endured the ultimate suffering, betrayal, torture and death, but yet still gained eternal life in Heaven with our Father, should reassure you too that this shall pass. The righteous suffer. That's just a fact of life. I won't promise you that all you have to do is have a close relationship with God, pray, and have faith for your problems to go away. The bible says that, "Through many tribulations we must enter the kingdom of God (Acts 14:22)."

Even as I sit here in my purpose and calling, being obedient to the Lord by writing this book, all hell is breaking lose. The kids are having tantrums, my head is killing me, checks that are supposed to come haven't made it yet, unexpected expenses are popping up all over the place, but yet I march on. I do so because I've learned to thrive in the middle of a storm. If I don't, life will pass me right on by while I sit paralyzed by the rain.

Knowing that you will always have trouble in this world, the real question is, will you choose fear or faith? Will you rest in Gods ability to lead you along the perfect path that he has carved out for your life or will you be afraid and instead try to take matters into your own hands? Fear is the enemy whispering in your ear, "God won't do what he said he will do. You are alone and there is no one to help you get through this." But, do you really believe that?

There have been so many times over the past several years where I was faced with a choice to have faith or be afraid. It is a choice. You don't just pray for faith. That's why the bible tells us that, "Without faith, it is impossible to please

God, because anyone who comes to him must believe that he exists and that he rewards those who earnestly seek him (Hebrews 11:6)."

Your faith says that even though you're afraid, that you are coming to God in the belief that he already has this worked out for your good. You seek God first in the storm, do what he tells you to, and then you rest in his ability to get you through this.

When we lost our last car to repossession, I remember an instant feeling of fear come over me. But, in that moment I had a choice to believe that we wouldn't be ok or I had a choice to believe that God would somehow work this out for our good. I chose faith. I chose faith because I had already seen all of the many things that God brought me through. I realized in that moment that life would always throw situations at us which require that choice. What's ironic is the only way to continue to strengthen our faith is to continuously be placed in situations that only God can get us out of.

Whether you agree with me or not, I know that God is at the very center of your loss. I've heard people tell me that God never takes away,

He only gives, gives, gives. Although there is some truth to that, God knows every single thing that is going on in your life. Believe me, if he didn't have a purpose in this, it would not be happening. Remember too that the enemy will always try to capitalize anywhere he can. If he thinks you're doing bad, he will try his best to make it worse. But God will, somehow, even use that for your good.

"It was good for me to be afflicted so that I might learn your decrees. The law from your mouth is more precious to me than thousands of pieces of silver and gold. Your hands made me and formed me; give me understanding to learn your commands. May those who fear you rejoice when they see me, for I have put my hope in your word. I know, Lord, that your laws are righteous, and that in faithfulness you have afflicted me (Psalm 119:71-75)."

If you can keep in mind at all times that the Lord is at the center of your loss, getting through the days won't be as tough. Knowing that the God who controls the entire universe is aware of and magically orchestrating everything for your good should reassure you that everything will be just fine.

Have peace in the midst of this storm. Peace is just as much of a choice as faith is. You are only guaranteed this very moment you're in. Whoever promised you that you would be here to see your children graduate, your grandchildren born, or your retirement sitting on a rocking chair enjoying the birds chirping one day, was lying to you. I hate to sound harsh but it just isn't true.

Almost every day, I hear of a child, young mother, or father of three who have died in some horrific manner. Between cancer, car accidents, the economy and violence, none of us are exempt. You have *this* moment to be happy, praise God, and be better. You have *this* moment to hug your children tightly and sit at the park in awe of life's little mysteries. Don't take for granted the beauty of *this* moment because you are so caught up in what you've lost or how far you think you have to go. What matters is now.

While you are in the midst of this storm, God is trying to draw you closer to him. He loves you, cherishes your time and worship towards him and wants to have an intimate relationship with you. Right now, while you aren't so distracted by your material possessions or partner, he can talk to you, tell you his plans for your life, refine your heart, and strengthen your faith. This time of relying on the Lord to get you through will prove to be one of the most intense and rewarding times of your life.

I tell my husband often that I am so grateful for every single thing we lost. If I had to do it all over again, I would without the blink of an eye. If God saw fit to take me through this valley again, I would happily go. I say that because of the relationship I now have with him. Where I once was a part time Christian, I am now devoted to Lord on a full time basis. Where I once lived a life of destructive sin, I now try my best to live honorably, and where I once had a heart that was self-focused, I now have a heart that is focused on serving the Lord. Life has more meaning and my relationship with God is far deeper than I could have ever known before.

Make it your mission right now to get to know everything about God that you can. Chances are, as you begin to bounce back from your loss, you won't have or make the kind of time for him that you have now. I'm not saying for you to sit down with the bible and read the entire thing in a month! However, if you are that inspired, by all means, don't let me keep you from it.

For me, I wanted to better know the stories of the bible; it's history and characters. All I really knew of God was what I learned at church. While that is certainly a start, don't let the only thing you know of God be what someone else tells you about him. As I began to read more about what he did for his people through the history of the bible, I began to trust him more to direct my path as well. God spoke to me during those intimate times of worship, prayer and praise. The promises he spoke to me during those dark times in my life are coming to pass in the light. He wants to do the same for you.

Even in the midst of this storm, you are blessed. If you don't get anything I have said in this entire book, please get that. Stop and think about all of the times from birth through now that God has saved you from something. Write at least one thing down and raise your hands towards heaven and give God the glory for what he has done for you!

When I was 5 years old, I lived in Washington State with my Dad and stepmother for a short time. Two weeks before I was supposed to go on the road with my (truck driver) dad for the summer, my mother called and wanted me home. Unfortunately, that truck crashed killing my stepmother and severely injuring my dad. Had I been in the cab, unbuckled and as tiny as I was, there is no doubt that I would have been dead. I just praise God now for grace and protection!

I honestly believe that being grateful for what we had left was the key that unlocked the blessings God had in store for us. But, even more than that, I believe God has blessed us because he knew that he could trust us to be a blessing to others. See, God not only wants the best *for* you but he wants to *use* you to bring hope, encouragement, and resources to the people around you.

How many people have you heard say that they would pray for someone? A lot, I'm sure.

Now, how many times have you heard people say, "God bless the homeless, sick, widow or orphans?" I would dare to say even more. So, let me ask you this, who do you think he wants to use to bless all of these discouraged people? Yes, that's right, he wants to use you.

Jesus gives us two simple commands, "Love the Lord your God with all your heart and with all your soul and with all your strength and with all your mind; and Love your neighbor as yourself (Luke 10:27)." If you were lying on the concrete in the middle of down town, alone, hungry and dirty, I'm sure you would feed yourself right? Silly question. So, why aren't you feeding the homeless? God wants to use you to love your neighbors; not just with encouraging words and prayers but also with material resources. The blessings he has for you are not just for you.

While you are going through this season of loss, focus on being a good steward of your money. If you don't have to buy a brand new car, brand new clothes or eat out every night, then don't. I kid you not, my husband and I still to this very day go on craigslist to find something we need before we run to a store and buy it new. Once we recognized that God wanted to use us to bless others, we tried to find ways in order to be better stewards of the money he trusted us with.

Right now, I am sitting on a used bed, typing on my used Apple computer, looking out on my back porch at the used patio furniture that is sitting on a used outdoor rug. Before I lost everything I owned, you wouldn't have caught me dead telling you that (because it wouldn't happen). Now, I better understand that everything I own and every penny I have in the bank is God's and if I want him to continue to bless me, I better make sure I am spending it in a manner which honors him and his kingdom.

God wants you to prosper. He wants to bless you and give you all the things he has in store for you. I think we do a good job today in our churches preaching that with a loud speaker. But, what gets left out is that he doesn't want you to prosper for your own selfish gain but to serve him first.

There were quite a few times of testing that I went through while losing everything. I can vividly remember one time when we only had about $100 in the bank to last us a couple of weeks. It was a very scarce amount to try and buy food and gas for a family of 4 and one on the way. I had a very dear family member call me crying to tell me they had no food. Right at that moment, God placed it in my spirit to give that person half of what we had. He just said, "Trust me." So, I was obedient with his money. That next week, my husband ended up getting a call for a job and everything was ok.

I truly believe God was testing our family in those moments of lack. In fact, I know he was because he says in his word that, "Whoever can be trusted with very little can also be trusted with much, and whoever is dishonest with very little will also be dishonest with much (Luke 16:10)." I don't know how much more "little" you can get than giving away ½ of $100 with nothing in sight for weeks!

There were many more times over the course of the last several years where God tested us in our giving. Time after time, he asked us to buy sleeping bags for the homeless, send a mother a large amount of money to help bury her small child, send cash to someone who was about to be kicked out of their apartment, or money to a mother who needed to take her child for medical treatments. Each time, we responded without hesitation, with obedience, and cheerfully because we knew what it was like to have little. But, God always gave us back way more than what we could ever give to him. "Whoever is kind to the poor, lends to the Lord, and he will reward them for what they have done (Proverbs 19:17)" God just wants to know if he can use you to flow blessings through you.

Continuously be on the lookout for ways you can meet the need of others. God tells us many times in the bible to care for the poor, widows, and orphans. Be obedient to that. You don't have to wait to join a ministry at church to help someone else. Be on the lookout daily and also stay in prayer over whom you should help. You won't be able to do everything but don't let that keep you from doing something. God has always placed in my spirit or in my path someone who is in need of encouragement, love, prayer or material support. He will do the same for you.

If you weren't actively and obediently giving back to God before your loss, I would tell you that this is one of the most important things he wants you to master. In fact, if you don't give back to God through tithes and offering, you are robbing him and breaking his promises with you. Malachi chapter 3 says:

"Will a mere mortal rob God? Yet you rob me. But you ask, 'How are we robbing you?'

"In tithes and offerings. You are under a curse—your whole nation—because you are robbing me. Bring the whole tithe into the storehouse, that there may be food in my house. Test me in this," says the Lord Almighty, "and see if I will not throw open the floodgates of heaven and pour out so much blessing that there will not be room enough to store it. I will prevent pests from devouring your crops, and the vines in your fields will not drop their fruit before it is ripe," says the Lord Almighty. "Then all the nations will call you blessed, for yours will be a delightful land," says the Lord Almighty (Malachi 3:8-12)."

Don't let greed rob you of the real blessings God has for you. By letting go of what you believe is yours and instead saying, "Lord, what do you want me to do with this money," God will honor your obedience with more. When you learn to detach yourself from things, you keep what's truly important at the forefront of your mind and heart and that's God.

As I sit here in this beautiful home on over an acre of beautiful land with two new vehicles in the driveway, credit on the way up, money in the bank, two children in private school and the ability to walk in a grocery store and buy what I *want* instead of what I *need*, I am just amazed at God's goodness. But, what I am more amazed at is the person I am now who walks in purpose.

Since going through my loss, God has blessed our family enough financially to be able to give away thousands to people who are hurting, discouraged and in need. But, what's incredible about that, to me, is not so much that I can give away money but more so that God is using me to answer someone's prayer. When I go to someone by the leading of the Holy Spirit and say, "God sent me with this. He wanted me to tell you that he loves you and has you in the palm of his hands," the feeling of joy overwhelms me. I always say that blesses *me* more than it does *them.*

What you are going through right now will help someone else. I've heard people say you will "lead where you bleed." Now, I understand that. Just by being completely transparent with my imperfection as a human being and sharing what God has done through such a flawed sinner like me, thousands have been encouraged. I pray even millions are encouraged as this book reaches the hands of those who need it.

By me leading the way, through God's direction to help the homeless in our city, there are now regular groups and churches that meet every month downtown and bring hope, encouragement and material resources to the forgotten. Most importantly, they bring Jesus with them. Prayer, laughter and love show up in a dark place. I would like to think its what real ministry is like, the one that models the life of Jesus. In some small way, I'm proud that I am just a little responsible for a tiny bit of good that is now being done to bring glory to God. But, I never would be here, helping anyone, showing people a glimpse of Jesus and leading them to him had I never went through this journey.

Your loss is much bigger than you. It's a series of perfectly orchestrated events that when used for the glory of God will draw the lost and discouraged into the kingdom. God called you by name before he ever placed you in your mother's womb. He needs you to use the pain of this time in your life to ignite a passion for a calling bigger than yourself that will push you into your purpose! The path is already established but the, "...gate is small and the way is narrow that leads to life, and there are few who find it (Matthew 7:13)." Will you be one of them? Will you hear what God is saying to you and bounce back or will you lie down and give up in the wilderness? The promised land awaits, but more importantly, destiny awaits, are you ready?...

Let me leave you with some encouragement...

Where I Grew Up

What I Earned & Lost

What God Gave Me for My Trouble!!!

But, What Matters the Most…Giving Back

If this book encouraged or inspired you in any way, please share it with others. You never know who may need it now or in the future.

I would love to hear from you! You can connect with me the following ways:

Website   www.ILostEverything.com

www.Twitter.com/StephLynnKing

www.Facebook.com/AuthorSLK